Also by Gerry Adams

Before the Dawn

Cage Eleven

Falls Memories

Free Ireland: Towards a Lasting Peace

Hope and History

An Irish Journal

An Irish Voice

The New Ireland

A Pathway to Peace

The Politics of Irish Freedom

Selected Writings

The Street and Other Stories

Who Fears to Speak...?

GW00771615

MY LITTLE BOOK OF
TWEETS

GERRY ADAMS

MERCIER PRESS
IRISH PUBLISHER – IRISH STORY

MERCIER PRESS

Cork

www.mercierpress.ie

© Gerry Adams, 2016

ISBN: 978 1 78117 449 4

10 9 8 7 6 5 4 3 2 1

A CIP record for this title is available from the British Library.

Printed and bound in the EU.

Note:

Every effort has been made to trace the copyright holders of material used, and to obtain their permission for the use of copyright material. If, despite our efforts to prevent such an occurrence, the use of any material is a breach of copyright, we apologise sincerely and will be more than happy to incorporate the relevant notice in future reprints or editions of this book.

For the little people in my life.
Le grá mór do Dhrithle, Luisne,
Anna agus Ruadan.

Do Mary O'Herlihy
xoxo

Corcaigh 2016

Reamhrá

His tweets have been described as bizarre, weird and conversely as part of a clever and subversive republican strategy. They have also provided acres of newsprint and endless broadcasting material for the chattering classes. The tweets themselves have been analysed forensically along with the person behind them.

We cannot speak for him but he is our friend and it appears to us that he sees tweeting as a democratic process of communication.

After all there is no editorial middle person to say what he or she feels you might have said or what they think you meant. Not a lot of space for misrepresentation. No censorship. No, when you tweet that's it. No moderator to filter the message through. Tweeting is also immediate.

Maybe that's why some of Gerry Adams' detractors in the media are so obsessed by his twitterings. He has moved beyond them and is finding an audience which is no longer dependent on the establishment media for its information and opinions.

But his tweets are not just about politics and polemic though that is part of what he does.

They are not just about information though there is that also.

They are about life as he sees it. As it happens. And OK, he might have his own way of looking at things but that can't be bad and at least he doesn't take himself too seriously. Most of the time. And he is not afraid to act the eejit.

Some of the time.

So there is music and sport and food, friends and family, the natural world and maybe the supernatural world also.

That and dogs and plastic ducks and Teddy bears. Which is where we come in.

We are just glad to get our rightful place in the scheme of things. That's why we like Gerry's *Little Book of Tweets*.

This selection is almost devoid of party politics. It is a mix of observations and adventure, wry commentary and random twitterings.

The first three tweets published here are what brought this side of our friend's life to the attention of the Twitter community. It happened when our other friend RG went off with the keys of their abode.

That's when this Twitter account took on a life of its own. We are glad it did. This little book is a sample of some of the saner tweets. A few slightly amended. We hope you enjoy it.

    If nothing else it's a wee bit of craic. *Bain sult as.**

Tom and Ted.

October 2015

* Enjoy

Buíochas

Mo buíochas le Drithle go háirithe, agus Máire, Séamus, RG, Aidan, Dennis. Thanks to Sarah, Mary and Deirdre at Mercier Press.

Buíochas also to Máire T, Áine T, Emma, RG, Charlie, Leslie, Paula, Hugh Russell, Markie Marks, Peadar and Róisín, Alan Lewis Photopress; Minnie, Aisling and Gavin for their photos. Thanks also to everyone who sent rubber ducks or tweets to my Twitter account.

https://twitter.com/GerryAdamsSF

https://www.facebook.com/gerryadams.sf

http://www.leargas.blogspot.ie

Gerry Adams @GerryAdams SF 8 Feb 2013

RG took the car, took my keys also.
I feel an adventure coming on.

Gerry Adams @GerryAdams SF 8 Feb 2013

RG's phone constantly engaged, it's
getting darker.
I would climb in back window but
downpipe broken.

Gerry Adams @GerryAdams SF 8 Feb 2013

RG traced. Where are you now when we need you? 70 miles away. I'm starving. Need a glazier. *Slán.**

* Goodbye

Gerry Adams @GerryAdams SF 12 Feb 2013

In the Dáil chamber. Thought I had a pen in my pocket discovered it is a toothbrush!

Gerry Adams @GerryAdams SF 6 May 2013

Snowie Adams. A mighty dog for one dog.

Gerry Adams @GerryAdams SF 15 Feb 2013

Friday. Getting home.

Gerry Adams @GerryAdams SF 11 Aug 2014

I've tons of dishes 2 wash. Shudda
done them last night. Ah so ...
*Maidin maith daoibhse.**

* Good morning all!

Gerry Adams @GerryAdams SF 27 Jan 2015

Still in the Dáil chamber, boringggggg. Seán Crowe has joined me, cheered me up. He sez Crowes don't tweet. Caw Caw.

 Gerry Adams @GerryAdams SF 29 Jan 2015

1st pilates of the year *deanta agam*,* tough. *Tiocfaidh Ár* Aaaaaagggghhhhhh!

* done by me

Gerry Adams @GerryAdams SF 14 Jun 2014

How do you hollow out an orange?

Gerry Adams @GerryAdams SF 25 Jun 2014

In bed with Tom Jones, Van
Morrison and Doris Day, Pavarotti
and Planxty.

Gerry Adams @GerryAdams SF 29 Jan 2015

Snow joke being a Louth fox.

Gerry Adams @GerryAdams SF 21 Jul 2014

Thank God we're surrounded by water.

Gerry Adams @GerryAdams SF 5 Feb 2015

The fox he came a courting.
Our Louth fox has come back with
a friend.

Gerry Adams @GerryAdams SF 5 Feb 2015

New ducks, a whole flock. xo

Gerry Adams @GerryAdams SF

Wee buns.

Gerry Adams @GerryAdams SF 5 Feb 2015

Smaghetti 2night, garlic bread and olive oil. I love olive oil.

Gerry Adams @GerryAdams SF 11 Feb 2015

I have 2 hoover the bathroom and wash the dishes, empty the washing machine, iron a shirt and soak RG's porridge b4 *leaba.** Just saying.

* bed

Gerry Adams @GerryAdams SF 20 Jun 2014

How do they know it's Friday night? All sitting waiting for me to fill the bath with soapy suds and Epsom salts.

Tom & Ted Time.

Gerry Adams @GerryAdams SF 9 Feb 2015

It's cold in them there hills, only way
2 start the week!

Gerry Adams @GerryAdams SF 16 Feb 2015

Spring is springing, primroses and 1st sign of daffodils and Fionn is bigger than Nuada. *Anois ar theacht an tSamhraidh.**

* Now the summer is coming.

Gerry Adams @GerryAdams SF 15 Jan 2015

A windblown girl, intent on reading her book, strides along the pavement. Oblivious to the weather she marches schoolwards through the storm.

Gerry Adams @GerryAdams SF 08 Jan 2015

Thinking may sometimes be overrated.

Gerry Adams @GerryAdams SF 10 Jan 2015

I measc na sléibhte ar an lá fhuar geal seo. * Cavehill from Sliabh Dubh and Béal Feirste from high ground.

* Among the mountains on this cold, clear day. Cavehill from Black Mountain and Belfast from high ground.

Gerry Adams @GerryAdams SF 10 Feb 2015

A Dáil Day.

WARNING
QUICKSAND

Gerry Adams @GerryAdams SF 05 Jan 2015

I'm sitting out in the duskiness of the evening drinking a bottle of Decadence Stout, listening 2 the wind playing with the trees.

Gerry Adams @GerryAdams SF 21 Sep 2014

Sam is for the Hills. There will not be
a sheep milked in Donegal tonight.

Gerry Adams @GerryAdams SF 06 Jul 2014

If you think you can't you won't.
If you think you can you will.

Gerry Adams @GerryAdams SF 18 Jan 2015

First outing on new bike.

Gerry Adams @GerryAdams SF 01 Jan 2015

What height was Elvis?

Gerry Adams @GerryAdams SF 31 Dec 2014

Just back banjaxed, hungry, soaked and sweating. 2 many layers. But the walk was *iontach*,* our country is very beautiful. So am I.

* wonderful

Gerry Adams @GerryAdams SF 16 Feb 2013

Left Ted in BAC.* Methinks RG hid him. Jealousy. Hope he is ok. Miss him 2night. Long but good oul day. Can't find my ipad either. Ted have it? zzz

* (*Baile Átha Cliath*) Dublin

Gerry Adams @GerryAdams SF 16 Feb 2013

Sorry RG *mea culpa*.* Ted just phoned. He is in Bfast also. He has a date. Wants u 2 pick him up 2mara after Mass. He says u know where? *Slán.* xo

* my fault

Gerry Adams @GerryAdams SF 17 Feb 2013

Ted turned up. Safe and sound. He spent the night with Tom. Tom is nice. A *gaeilgeoir.** Plays *bodhrán*. Wants 2 move in. I'm ok with this. RG is iffy.

* Irish-speaking enthusiast

Gerry Adams @GerryAdams SF 08 Aug 2013

Ye take the high road.

Gerry Adams @GerryAdams SF 14 Jun 2014

Ally bally, ally bally bee, sitting on your daideo's knee, lukin 4 a wee bobbin 2 buy some Coulter's candy.

Gerry Adams @GerryAdams SF 15 Jun 2014

My garden is inclusive, here's the other lily. They all live happily *le chéile*,* blooming brilliant no borders.

* together

Gerry Adams @GerryAdams SF 18 Jun 2014

Little people in my life showing how 2 shorten a journey.

Gerry Adams @GerryAdams SF 26 Apr 2015

Tom and Ted waiting for *Voice of Ireland* result.

Gerry Adams @GerryAdams SF 21 Jun 2014

I fumbled in my bag 4 clean Y fronts, pulled out the baby's bib instead. Silly Billy. Need to pack better in future.

Gerry Adams @GerryAdams SF 20 Jun 2014

De early bee gets de honey.

Gerry Adams @GerryAdams SF 03 Jul 2014

Well at least something good came outta my visit to London. Best thing to come from British Parliament to Ireland?

Gerry Adams @GerryAdams SF 20 Jun 2014

Off 2 BAC.* Tom and Ted coming with me, they love BAC. This is why.

* *(Baile Átha Cliath) Dublin*

Gerry Adams @GerryAdams SF 20 Jun 2014

I made roast chicken, roast garlic, Comber spuds, corn and broccoli. *An dheas,** wee dogs 4 dessert, scrumptious.

* Very nice

Gerry Adams @GerryAdams SF 03 Jul 2014

Tick Tocky *Ár Lá*.*

* Our day

Gerry Adams @GerryAdams SF 20 Jun 2014

Red is the rose that in yonder garden grows, fair is the lily of the valley, but my love is fairer than any. Zzzoxozz.

Gerry Adams @GerryAdams SF 16 Dec 2014

A tree is for life. Not just for Christmas.

Gerry Adams @GerryAdams SF 26 Jun 2014

Me, Emma, Pádraig, Fintan, and Oscar have a wee look at SF proposals 4 LGBT EQUALITY. Nothing 2 declare but our commitment, BRÓD.*

* Pride

Gerry Adams @GerryAdams SF 09 May 2014

Bluebells are for love sez Patrick
Kavanagh.

Gerry Adams @GerryAdams SF 29 Jun 2014

1 of my favourite *Deoirín Dé* – God's tears or fuchsia in the Pale. Legends said Jesus' tears dropped on to the leaves.

Gerry Adams @GerryAdams SF 21 Feb 2013

Out on bike b4 dawn. A choir
of blackbirds lightened me and
brightened the day. Met a woman in
pink PJs. Walking a one-legged dog.
Odd.

Gerry Adams @GerryAdams SF 02 Jul 2014

Well done 2 Christy and others 4 getting the Arthur's Day (Arthur Guinness) scrapped, just goes to show that these big companies don't like controversy.

Gerry Adams @GerryAdams SF 02 Jul 2014

Funny incident in BAC* airport, I tried walking through a glass panel, guy on the other side was quite startled. So was I.

(Baile Átha Cliath) Dublin

Gerry Adams @GerryAdams SF 30 Jun 2014

Out 4 a dander b4 bed, spied this mammy heron out fishing 4 dindins. Herons r funny old birds.

Gerry Adams @GerryAdams SF 08 Jul 2014

An interesting extract from a British
Government secret file from 1978,
just saying.

CONFIDENTIAL ~~COYEFIDE~~ SECRET

I attach all the papers I can lay my hands on regarding Adams.
These files, SM 1602 and SCA 715, were the records kept by the
now defunct Division 2(B) and the equally defunct office of the
advisers respectively.

The following is a summary of Adams' detention history which I
hope might save you wading through the files too much.

1.	14.03.72	Arrested under Regulation 11(1) of the Civil Authorities (Special Powers) Act (WI) 1922.
2.	15.03.72	Detained under Regulation 11(2) of the CASPA.
3.	20.04.72	Recommended for internment under Regulation 12 of the CASPA (not approved).

Gerry Adams @GerryAdams SF 05 Mar 2013

This is a magical morning. *Iontach*.*
Out on the *rothar*.* On a high. Saw
the woman with the one-legged dog
again. He never gives up she sez.

* wonderful
* bicycle

Gerry Adams @GerryAdams SF 22 Jun 2014

Hurling is the best game in the
world.

Gerry Adams @GerryAdams SF 12 Jul 2014

The standard of hurling this year is 90, Clare didn't deserve to lose. But neither did Wexford, great game!

Gerry Adams @GerryAdams SF 13 Jul 2014

The Black Mountain, Sliabh Dubh
speaks.

Gerry Adams @GerryAdams SF 06 Dec 2014

Relic of the British rule in Palestine, just like Dundalk or Dublin.

Gerry Adams @GerryAdams SF 06 Oct 2015

I really like sitting outside under shelter with the rain blathering down!

Gerry Adams @GerryAdams SF 04 Feb 2015

Flatulence is a curse.

Gerry Adams @GerryAdams SF 25 Dec 2014

These wee ducks slipped in.

Gerry Adams @GerryAdams SF 20 Jul 2014

2nd oldest little person in my life asked me 'Are there police in Gaza? Can they stop the soldiers?'

Gerry Adams @GerryAdams SF 25 Jan 2014

Dreamt I was eating Cream Eggs. Woke up this morn. Pillow and beard covered in chocolate and cream thingybob.

Gerry Adams @GerryAdams SF 16 Jul 2014

At swim two birds.

Gerry Adams @GerryAdams SF 02 Aug 2014

The mountain speaks, *arís*!*

* again

Gerry Adams @GerryAdams SF 14 Feb 2014

Standing at the corner in the rain watching all the girls go by. Standing at the corner in Dundalk in the rain giving all the girls the eye.

Gerry Adams @GerryAdams SF 02 Aug 2014

New mural 4 big Doc at Slemish Way in Atown.*

* Andersonstown

Gerry Adams @GerryAdams SF 06 Aug 2014

I came upon this model of the H Block. Isn't it a wonderment the things you can come upon?

Gerry Adams @GerryAdams SF 05 Aug 2014

Well done Ireland's women's rugby team, a great victory!

Gerry Adams @GerryAdams SF 12 Jun 2014

When you come to the end of a lollipop. To the end. To the end of a lollipop. When you come to the end of a lollipop. Pop goes your heart. xo

From the song 'When you come to the end of a lollipop' – Max Bygraves

Gerry Adams @GerryAdams SF 10 Aug 2014

I never took to eating crisps. Athletes don't.

Gerry Adams @GerryAdams SF 13 Aug 2014

Did I ever tell you I'm allergic to midgies. I swell up.

Gerry Adams @GerryAdams SF 16 Feb 2014

A Saint Bernard dog just sidled up to the sofa and gave me a brandy and port. Nuada and Snowie never even barked. Hope he comes back. Or am I dreaming?

Gerry Adams @GerryAdams SF 19 Aug 2014

I have an appointment with a horse.
Hi Ho Silver away.

Gerry Adams @GerryAdams SF 07 Oct 2015

The Sinn Féin Style Police pulled me in earlier. Apparently I was reported for the length of my beard. They gave me 24 hours to get it cut.

Gerry Adams @GerryAdams SF 20 Aug 2014

A morning selfie with Jenny or as she says a goatee with Gerry, *maidin mhaith daoibh.**

* good morning to you

Gerry Adams @GerryAdams SF 18 Aug 2014

I love dark chocolate.

Gerry Adams @GerryAdams SF 17 Feb 2013

Yes Tom & Ted are a same sex couple. But that's their business.

Gerry Adams @GerryAdams SF 22 Feb 2014

I feel like a Duvet Day.

Gerry Adams @GerryAdams SF 19 Aug 2014

When you lose yet another *sliothar.**

* hurling ball

Gerry Adams @GerryAdams SF 26 Aug 2014

On top of Errigal it's all downhill from here!

Gerry Adams @GerryAdams SF 26 Jan 2014

Everyone else got a strawberry on their pavlova except me. Why?

Gerry Adams @GerryAdams SF 27 Feb 2014

Got a flashback to the one-legged dog. Saw a two-legged cat. Walking very tall in Pearse Street. On hind legs.

Gerry Adams @GerryAdams SF 24 Aug 2014

The only way to bate bad breath!

Gerry Adams @GerryAdams SF 19 Jul 2014

The last time I was in Palestine.
I wonder did these young ones
survive the latest onslaught? *Maidin
Mhaith.**

* Good morning

Gerry Adams @GerryAdams SF 28 Apr 2014

I was born with a beard, I stopped shaving when I was 3.

Gerry Adams @GerryAdams SF 15 Jul 2014

Pilates, aaaaaahhhhhh

Gerry Adams @GerryAdams SF 07 Sep 2014

Russell with his dummy,
I blame his mummy.

Gerry Adams @GerryAdams SF 27 Dec 2014

A secret squirrel spying on me and Nuada during our walk.

Gerry Adams @GerryAdams SF 27 Dec 2014

I shook off the secret squirrel then spotted this crowd following me. I'm ducked.

Gerry Adams @GerryAdams SF 30 Oct 2013

Rain rain go away, this is mammy's washing day.

Gerry Adams @GerryAdams SF 11 Sep 2014

This is a carrot I met earlier.

Gerry Adams @GerryAdams SF 07 Aug 2013

Je suis fatigué ach chuir the little people in my life the *fáilte fhlaithúil romhaim** – suds and ducks galore xoxozzz.

* I am tired but the little people in my life had a great welcome for me

Gerry Adams @GerryAdams SF 25 Sep 2014

The dreaded 4 SSSS selected for special security search or some such surveillance. Impedes my exit. Free New York 1.

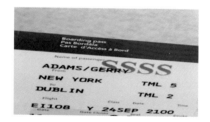

Gerry Adams @GerryAdams SF 09 Oct 2014

Hands up who will be voting for Sinn Féin?

Image © National Library of Ireland

Gerry Adams @GerryAdams SF 09 Oct 2014

Hands up who else will be voting for
Sinn Féin?

Gerry Adams @GerryAdams SF 08 Jul 2015

With James Connolly Heron, great grandson of 1916 James Connolly. Campaigning to save the 1916 battlefield site at Moore Street beside the GPO.

Gerry Adams @GerryAdams SF 27 Oct 2014

One of the great things about a beard is you get a taste of dinner for ages afterwards. Same with chocolate or a pint. Just saying, oichey oichey xozzzz.

Gerry Adams @GerryAdams SF 01 Nov 2015

Fair play to everyone who marched for right2water, it was a great day. *Ní neart go cur le chéile. Leanaigí ar aghaidh.**

* There is no strength without unity. Keep going.

Gerry Adams @GerryAdams SF 09 Nov 2014

Isn't it funny that I feel chuffed cos I figured out the end of *Love/Hate*? Columbo that's me. Or Inspector Clouseau?

Gerry Adams @GerryAdams SF 21 Nov 2014

I am not and I never have been a member of Isis.

Gerry Adams @GerryAdams SF 14 Dec 2014

Time for a hot soapy sudsy soak.

Gerry Adams @GerryAdams SF 16 Dec 2014

Government TDs voting for water services bill. Very festive turkeys. Or are they just chicken?

Gerry Adams @GerryAdams SF 17 Jun 2013

I will get by with a little help from my friends.

Gerry Adams @GerryAdams SF 16 Dec 2014

Sinn Féin Twitter Police say I shouldn't tweet this picture of the Oireachtas Christmas tree.

Gerry Adams @GerryAdams SF 15 Sep 2013

I used to sing 'Black Velvet Band' at the top of my voice while cycling to Glenavy. I once got so carried away that I cycled into a field.

Gerry Adams @GerryAdams SF 01 Jan 2014

All you need is love, all you need is love, all you need is love, love is all you need.
An grá abú!*

* Love forever
From the song 'All You Need Is Love' – Beatles

Gerry Adams @GerryAdams SF 23 Sep 2014

'I do like David Attenborough,' he whispered from the undergrowth. 'So do I,' said Lonesome George.

Gerry Adams @GerryAdams SF 10 Jun 2015

You are my sunshine my only sunshine you make me happy when skies are grey, you will never know dear how much I love you please don't take my sunshine away.

From the song 'You Are My Sunshine'

Gerry Adams @GerryAdams SF 09 Feb 2013

Saw the breaking dawn, grey light.
Out on bike. Saw squirrel chasing a
cat, a grey one. The squirrel that is.
Glad to be alive. So is the cat.

Gerry Adams @GerryAdams SF 27 Dec 2013

My bestest pressie! The queen of all rubber ducks, a high class kinda ducky *ár lá** dee dah!

* our day

Gerry Adams @GerryAdams SF 22 Jul 2013

The hunger is on me now. A BIG
salad day methinks with fresh
melon for afters or befores!
Just a thought!

Gerry Adams @GerryAdams SF 04 Jun 2013

Got up this morning, feeling good got the happy blues the good feeling blues. This is the best day in my life blues, dat ain't bad.

Gerry Adams @GerryAdams SF 20 Feb 2015

Everything I do, I doooo it fooor uuuuh.

Gerry Adams @GerryAdams SF 10 Feb 2014

I wish I wish I wish in vain. I wish I was a youth again. But a youth again I never can be until apples grow on an ivy tree. Monday!!

Gerry Adams @GerryAdams SF 07 Jun 2014

Trimmed my beard, always make a balls of it. No patience, but at least it will grow again. *Codladh sámh** xo.

* Sleep well

Gerry Adams @GerryAdams SF 08 Jun 2014

My favourite rapper is meself.

Gerry Adams @GerryAdams SF 19 May 2015

So the bath beckons, plastic ducks, soapy suds *oíche mhaith codladh sámh** xo.

* good night sleep well

Gerry Adams @GerryAdams SF 12 Jun 2014

Seriously overstretched myself at pilates.

 Gerry Adams @GerryAdams SF 01 Jan 2014

I got the pre-budget blues, I sure have got them bad. I got the pre-budget blues the worst blues I ever have had. This govt is so bad I'm sad.

Gerry Adams @GerryAdams SF 19 Jan 2014

Out on bike this morning no hands,
look mammy no hands, exhilarating.
Lots of folks *ag rith, ag siúil.*
Iontach!*

* running, walking. Wonderful!

Gerry Adams @GerryAdams SF 26 Apr 2013

Dreamt I was in a café drinking coffee, Ryan Tubridy sat at my table, he smiled and read a newspaper. I was wearing one boot and one shoe. What does that mean?

Gerry Adams @GerryAdams SF 27 Dec 2013

Epsom salts *go deo*!*

* forever

Gerry Adams @GerryAdams SF 04 Jun 2013

'The more I learn about people the more I like my dog.' – Mark Twain.

'The more I learn about dogs the more I like my people.' – Snowie Adams.

Gerry Adams @GerryAdams SF 26 Oct 2014

Mrs Brown's Boys brought me back to reality after *Love/Hate*.

Gerry Adams @GerryAdams SF 23 Oct 2015

Too many Protestants. Too many
Catholics. Not enough Christians.

Gerry Adams @GerryAdams SF 01 Nov 2014

A man's gotta do what a man's gotta
do. Bring in the bins.

 Gerry Adams @GerryAdams SF 21 Feb 2015

So all is well in Enda land. No taxes!
Full employment. Emigrants back
home. Great public services. What a
spoof!! Call election Taoiseach.

Gerry Adams @GerryAdams SF 01 Sep 2014

This bloomed 2day, all on its own was on window 4 ages then ... *Go hálainn.**

* Beautiful

Gerry Adams @GerryAdams SF 16 Feb 2013

Got spuds and fruit in Moore St. *Craic mhaith*.* Molly Malones under p. Rates. Good coffee in SF Bookshop in Parnell Sq. *Tiocfaidh ár latte!!**

* Good fun

* Our latte will come!!

Gerry Adams @GerryAdams SF 15 Feb 2013

Luke Kelly, *fear iontach*,* singing 'Raglan Road' on radio. Makes me wanna cry. Poor Paddy Kavanagh. Best love poem ever. Best sung by Luke.

* wonderful man

Gerry Adams @GerryAdams SF 28 Sep 2014

There is a fly here really annoying me.

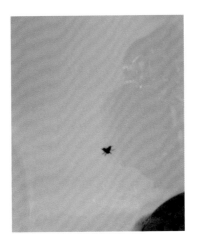

Gerry Adams @GerryAdams SF   10 Apr 2014

Remember Ireland's patriot dead.

Gerry Adams @GerryAdams SF 13 Oct 2014

Is Stormont sinking?

Gerry Adams @GerryAdams SF 22 Feb 2015

Ruadan's 1st *camán*.*
Croke Park here we come!!

* a hurl

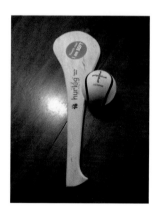

Gerry Adams @GerryAdams SF 26 Feb 2015

I found 'Aftershave' in the
bathroom. I have started 2 use it.
Even though I have no sense of
smell and I can't shave.

Gerry Adams @GerryAdams SF 27 Feb 2015

Little people in my life sent me a photo of Fionn. Waiting 4 me.
2 of us need a hug! Or a bounce!

Gerry Adams @GerryAdams SF 01 Mar 2015

A rainbow in S. Armagh. Camlough.
Just as Ireland bate England at
rugby.

Gerry Adams @GerryAdams SF 05 Mar 2015

One of the little people in my life and his friend.

Gerry Adams @GerryAdams SF

We lost. Again.

Gerry Adams @GerryAdams SF 09 Mar 2015

Drat! Left my Crocs in Derry!

Gerry Adams @GerryAdams SF 30 Jun 2015

Thought 4 bedtime. *Codladh Sámh**
xozzzzz.

* Sleep well

Gerry Adams @GerryAdams SF 10 Oct 2015

Visit The Ambassador. *Baile Átha Cliath*. From 27 Feb 2016. Celebrate & commemorate The Rising.

Gerry Adams @GerryAdams SF 14 Mar 2014

Got my Crocs back. They walked all the way home from Derry.

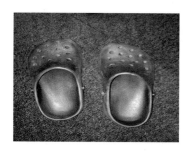

Gerry Adams @GerryAdams SF 28 Mar 2015

1 of the little people in my life with her Dalmatian.

Gerry Adams @GerryAdams SF 28 Mar 2015

U wud never know it but buddy I'm a kinda poet. Make it one 4 my baby and one more 4 the road. *Oíche mhaith** xoxozzzzzz.

* Good night

Gerry Adams @GerryAdams SF 16 Mar 2015

Still on the train. Chooo Chooo Choooo.

Are we there yet? Are we there yet?

Gerry Adams @GerryAdams SF 21 Nov 2015

Leabar beag iontach.
Go raibh maith agat. Seamus.

* Wonderful little book. Thank you.

Gerry Adams @GerryAdams SF 17 Mar 2015

At the Speaker's Lunch.

Gerry Adams @GerryAdams SF 21 Mar 2015

I love the fields of Athenry.
Especially in a Sports Stadium.

 Gerry Adams @GerryAdams SF 23 Mar 2015

Sometimes I wonder why.

Gerry Adams @GerryAdams SF 20 Mar 2015

My bath overflowth. Our 1st orange billed duck arrived 2night. A good suddy soak b4 zzzzzzzzz *Oíche mhaith*.* Xoxo

* Good night

Gerry Adams @GerryAdams SF 20 Mar 2015

Little and large.

Gerry Adams @GerryAdams SF 11 May 2015

Along the Boyne 2wards
Mornington. Spectacular sunset.

Gerry Adams @GerryAdams SF 21 Mar 2015

Great that Ireland won. Especially against Eggland.

Gerry Adams @GerryAdams SF 11 Feb 2015

And so 2 bed, *lá fada a bhí ann.
Mise scriosta ach sásta mar rinne
muid obair mhaith inniu. Oíche
mhaith agus codladh sámh.**
Xozzzzz

* it was a long day. I'm wrecked but pleased
because we got good work done today. Good
night and sleep well.

Gerry Adams @GerryAdams SF 21 Jan 2015

Dia daoibh.* Mr Hartley and I sang this fine song in C Wing in Belfast Prison and in a cell in RUC barracks. They threw us out. Last song at Niall Vallely's funeral mass. 'Sliabh Gallion Braes'.

* Hello [God be with you]

Final Song: *"Slieve Gallion Braes"*

As I was walkin' one morning all in the month of May
To view all your mountains and valleys so gay,
I was thinking on the flowers all going to decay
That bloom around ye, bonny, bonny Slieve Galleon Braes.

Full of times I have wandered with my dog and my gun,
I'd ramble these mountains and your valleys for fun,
But those days they now all over and I can no longer stay
So farewell unto you bonny, bonny, Slieve Galleon Braes.

How oft in the evening with the sun all in the west
I walked hand in hand with the one I love best
But the hopes of youth are ended and I am far away
So farewell unto you bonny bonny Slieve Galleon Braes

'tis not for the want of employment at home
That causes the son of ould Ireland to roam.
But the rates were gettin' higher and I could no longer stay
So farewell unto you bonny, bonny, Slieve Galleon Braes

Gerry Adams @GerryAdams SF 25 Jun 2015

Fionn ag éirí níos fearr agus Nuada sásta.*

* Fionn getting better and Nuada happy.

Gerry Adams @GerryAdams SF 25 Jan 2015

That's me 4th from the left of the Maidstone Prison ship. Spent some time there. Mostly locked below decks. *Áit dona.**

* A bad place

146

Gerry Adams @GerryAdams SF 23 Jun 2015

In bed with Johnny Cash, Engelbert Humperdinck, Maria Callas and Tom and Ted. *Oíche mhaith*.* xoxzzzzzzzz

* Good night

Gerry Adams @GerryAdams SF 23 Jun 2015

With Guard of Honour at Con
Colbert event in Athea. *NB* This is
not the Army Council. As far as I
know.

Gerry Adams @GerryAdams SF 28 Sep 2014

Got Leonard Cohen's new CD.
Iontach ar fad.* Oh me Oh My.
Leonard is a mighty man for one
man.

* Absolutely wonderful

Gerry Adams @GerryAdams SF 22 Oct 2015

At funerals for Traveller families, Lynch, Connors & Gilberts, killed in fire at Glenamuck. Jesus wept.

Gerry Adams @GerryAdams SF 09 Sep 2015

A big sheep in a field in Louth.

Gerry Adams @GerryAdams SF 23 Sep 2015

On the way to the ploughing with Mary Lou. With her floral water boots. Mine are pink.

Gerry Adams @GerryAdams SF 08 Oct 2015

The island of Ireland soccer teams won tonight. Well done to both teams. Time for one united team. A world beater.

Gerry Adams @GerryAdams SF 26 Oct 2014

Little people in my life demanding a
fry. Who am I to refuse them?

Gerry Adams @GerryAdams SF 26 Oct 2015

The more rugby games I watch the more I admire the players, especially our ones.

C'mon Ireland.

Gerry Adams @GerryAdams SF

Caught in the act. Martin Ferris takes ice cream from dog on a donkey. Only in the Kingdom.

Gerry Adams @GerryAdams SF 31 Mar 2015

The sun is shining. Shine with it.

Gerry Adams @GerryAdams SF 23 May 2015

@ Dublin Castle for Marriage Equality result. Selfie with Panti and Minister for Justice.

Comhionannas Abú!*

* Equality forever!

Gerry Adams @GerryAdams SF 10 Sep 2015

On way from Stormont 2 Ardee 4 a Fair Recovery meeting. I took wee walk. Love the Cooleys.

Gerry Adams ✔
@GerryAdamsSF

Sinn Féin President and TD for Louth

📍 County Louth   🔗 leargas.blogspot.com

756 FOLLOWING   **92K** FOLLOWERS

| Tweets | Media | Likes |

Slán.